Simple Slow Cooker Cookbook

Easy Crock Pot Recipes for Smart & Busy People

Best Recipes for Everyday Meals

by Colin Rivera

Table of Contents

INTRODUCTION 5

APPETIZERS 7

    Mexican Style Chili Colorado Burritos 7
    Delicious Parmesan-Crusted Chicken 9
    Simple BBQ Ribs 11
    Green Bean Casserole 12
    Classic Beef Lasagna 14
    Appetizing Chicken Caesar Sandwich 16
    Slow Cooker BBQ Chicken 18

MAIN DISHES 19

    Tender Beef and Broccoli 19
    Outstanding Sweet Pork 21
    Honey Chicken with Sesame Seeds 23
    Sweet Chicken Breast with Honey 25
    Famous Santa Fe Chicken 27
    Amazing Tender Chicken with Mushrooms 29
    Zucchini and Tomato Spicy Pasta Sauce 31
    Adorable Crockpot Italian Chicken 33
    Slow Cooker Hawaiian Chicken with Pineapple 34
    Bacon Cheese Potatoes 36
    Tender Pork Chops 37
    Delicious Chicken Cordon Bleu 39
    Tender Beef Stroganoff 40

SOUPS & STEWS 41

    German Classic Sauerkraut Soup 41
    Chicken Soup with Spinach and Herbs 43
    Mom's Amazing Pot Roast 45
    Salsa Verde Pork 46
    Potato Stew with Vegetables and Spices 47

COOKING MEASUREMENT CONVERSIONS 49

WAIT A MINUTE 52

CONCLUSION 53

Introduction

Greetings from Colin Rivera! I want to thank you for downloading my book "**Simple Slow Cooker Cookbook: Easy Crock Pot Recipes for Smart and Busy People – Best Recipes for Everyday Meals**"

This book contains a variety of ways and opportunities of how to increase the usage of the slow cooker for preparing healthy and tasty meals with minimal salt and oil.

The slow cooker became one of the most popular kitchen devices last time. Many people have crock pots on their kitchens but cook only one-two usual meals. That's why they do not know how to cook different dishes. If you are among them, throw away all doubts because there is a guide with perfect crock pot recipes you've ever seen!

Some people do not like to prepare meals in slow cookers because it takes so much time. But look on this from another side: at first, you can do any you want while meals are preparing, second – you do not need to use countless pot and skillets to cook dishes, all you need is to load all ingredients into your crock pot, switch it on and enjoy!

So do not hesitate and proceed to the study of 25 incredibly delicious, healthy and easy-to-prepare recipes.

Appetizers

Mexican Style Chili Colorado Burritos

Ingredients
- 1 ½ pound stew meat (beef)
- 1 can (18 oz) red enchilada sauce
- 2 beef bouillon cubes
- 1 can beans
- 6-8 burrito size tortillas
- 1 cup cheese (or more, depends on your preference), shredded.

Preparation
1. Cut beef into small pieces and put into the slow cooker.
2. Crush bouillon cubes over beef and add enchilada sauce.
3. Cook on low for at least 6 hours or until beef is very tender.
4. When meat is done, season to taste with salt and pepper.
5. Warm up beans.

6. Put couple teaspoons of beans in the center of each tortilla.
7. Add about ½ cup of beef and roll into a burrito.
8. Place burritos into a greased baking pan. Pour some extra sauce over the tops of the burritos to cover them. Place cheese on top.
9. Roast until cheese golden, maybe 2-4 minutes.

Delicious Parmesan-Crusted Chicken

Ingredients

- 2-3 chicken breasts, skinless
- ½ cup Italian seasoned breadcrumbs
- ¼ cup parmesan cheese, grated
- ¼ teaspoon ground black pepper
- ¼ teaspoon salt
- 1 tablespoon Olive oil
- 1 egg, beaten
- Sliced mozzarella cheese (optional)
- Favorite marinara sauce

Preparation

1. Sprinkle 1 tablespoon Olive Oil on the bottom of the slow cooker.
2. In a small bowl whisk the egg.
3. Mix Italian seasoned breadcrumbs, parmesan, ground pepper and salt in the middle bowl.
4. Dip the chicken into the egg and then into the breadcrumbs mixture. Evenly cover all sides of the chicken with egg and mixture.

5. Put the chicken breasts in the bottom of the crock pot.
6. Lay 3-4 slices of mozzarella cheese on top (optional).
7. Pour your favorite marinara sauce over chicken and cheese.
8. Close lid and prepare for low for 4-5 hours or until chicken becomes ready.
9. Serve with rice or pasta.

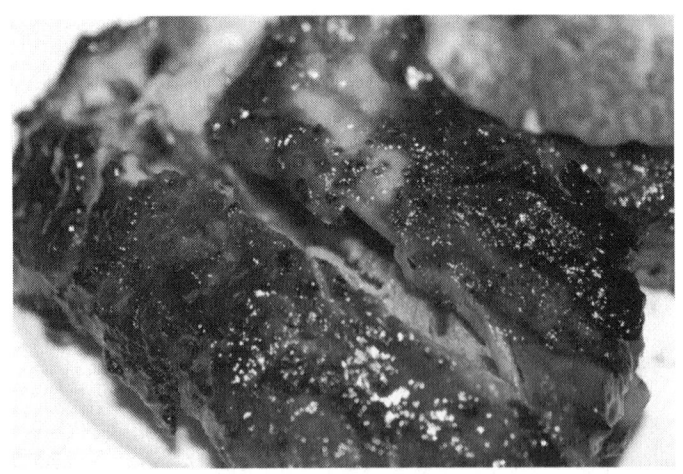

Simple BBQ Ribs

Ingredients

- 3 pounds pork loin ribs, boneless
- 3 tablespoon liquid smoke
- ½ cup brown sugar
- ½ cup sweet onion, diced
- 1 bottle (18 oz) favorite BBQ sauce

Preparation

1. Cover slow cooker with cooking spray.
2. Rub pork ribs with liquid smoke. Place them into the slow cooker.
3. Sprinkle brown sugar over the top of the ribs.
4. Pour the bottle of your favorite BBQ sauce over the of the ribs.
5. Cover and cook on low for 6-8 hours until ribs become tender.

Green Bean Casserole

Ingredients

- 2 can (15 oz) cut green beans, drained
- 1 can (10 oz) cream of mushroom soup, undiluted
- 1 package (8 oz) Cheddar cheese, shredded
- 5 oz fresh mushrooms, drained and sliced
- 1 cup milk
- 1 tablespoon Worcestershire sauce
- 1 can (6 oz) French fried onion rings, divided
- 1 teaspoon ground pepper
- Salt to taste

Preparation

1. In the large bowl combine green beans, mushroom soup, cheddar cheese, fresh mushrooms, milk, sauce and pepper.
2. Stir in half of French fried onion rings.
3. Grace slow cooker lightly and put casserole mixture into the crockpot.
4. Cover and cook on low for 2 hours.

5. Sprinkle remaining onion rings on the top of the dish, cover and cook another 30-40 minutes.

Classic Beef Lasagna

Ingredients

- 1 ground pound beef
- 1 jar (24 oz) Traditional Pasta Sauce
- 1 cup water
- 15 oz Original Ricotta Cheese
- 7 oz 2% milk shredded mozzarella cheese, divided
- ¼ cup parmesan cheese, grated and divided
- 1 egg
- 2 tablespoon fresh parsley, chopped
- 6 lasagna noodles, uncooked

Preparation

1. Brown ground beef a little in a large skillet, drain.
2. Stir in pasta sauce and water.
3. Combine 1 ½ cups ricotta, 2 tablespoon parmesan, egg and chopped parsley.
4. Put 1 cup meat mixture into the slow cooker, top with noodles (broken) and cheese mixture. Cover with 2

cups of meat mixture. Top with remaining noodles (broken), cheese and meat sauce.
5. Cover with lid and cook on low 4-6 hours, until liquid absorbed.
6. Then open, sprinkle with remaining cheeses and let stand covered up to 10 minutes until melted.

Appetizing Chicken Caesar Sandwich

Ingredients

- 2 pounds chicken breasts, boneless and skinless
- ½ cup Caesar dressing
- ½ cup parmesan cheese, shredded
- ¼ cup fresh parsley, chopped
- ½ teaspoon ground pepper
- 2 cups romaine lettuce, shredded
- 4-6 regular size hamburger buns

Preparation

1. Put chicken breasts into the slow cooker, pour 1-2 cups of water over, cover and cook on low for 4-5 hours.
2. Remove cooked chicken from the crockpot, drain the water from the slow cooker.
3. Shred the chicken using two forks and discarding any fat.
4. Place shredded chicken back to the slow cooker and pour dressing, parmesan cheese, parsley and pepper over.
5. Stir evenly.

6. Cover and cook for another 30 minutes or until ready.
7. Spoon the mixture into each slider bun.
8. Top with extra parmesan cheese and lettuce and serve.

Slow Cooker BBQ Chicken

Ingredients

- 1 ½ pounds chicken breasts, boneless and skinless
- 1 bottle favorite BBQ Sauce
- ¼ cup vinegar
- 1 teaspoon red pepper flakes
- 1 tablespoon brown sugar
- 1 teaspoon garlic powder

Preparation

1. Prepare chicken breasts.
2. In the middle bowl combine BBQ sauce, vinegar, red pepper flakes, brown sugar and garlic powder.
3. Place prepared chicken breasts to the slow cooker and pour the mixture over.
4. Cover and cook on low for 5-6 hours.
5. Enjoy!

Main Dishes

Tender Beef and Broccoli

Ingredients

- 1 pound beef chuck roast, sliced
- 1 cup beef broth
- ½ cup soy sauce
- 1/3 cup brown sugar
- 1 tablespoon sesame oil
- 3 garlic cloves, minced
- 2 tablespoons cornstarch
- 2 tablespoons water
- Fresh broccoli (as many as you like)
- Cooked rice

Preparation

1. Slice beef into thin strips.
2. Place meat in the crockpot.
3. In a middle bowl mix broth, soy sauce, brown sugar, sesame oil and garlic. Pour over beef.
4. Cover and cook on low for 6 hours.

5. In a little bowl stir cornstarch with water until smooth. Add to a slow cooker. Mix well.
6. Blanch broccoli and add to the crockpot. Stir to combine.
7. Cover and cook additionally for 20-25 minutes on high.
8. Serve with hot cooked rice.

Outstanding Sweet Pork

Ingredients
- 1.5-2 pounds pork
- 2 cans Coke (not diet)
- 1 teaspoon garlic salt
- ½ cup brown sugar
- ¼ cup water
- 1 can (4 oz) green chilies, diced
- 1 can (10 oz) enchilada sauce

Preparation
1. Take a large zip-lock bag and place the pork into it.
2. Add there 1 can of Coke, ½ cup of brown sugar. Make sure the pork dips into the marinade. Place the bag in the fridge for the whole night.
3. After that drain the marinade and put pork into the slow cooker.
4. Add ½ can of Coke, water and garlic salt over the meat.
5. Cook on high for at least 3-4 hours.
6. Once meat is almost ready shred it up with 2 forks.

7. Mix remaining Coke, green chilies, enchilada sauce and sugar in the large bowl.

Honey Chicken with Sesame Seeds

Ingredients

- 2-2.5 pounds skinless, boneless chicken breasts or thighs (as you wish)
- 1 cup honey
- ½ cup soy sauce
- 1 medium onion, diced
- 4 tablespoons ketchup or tomato sauce
- 2 tablespoons canola oil
- 2-3 cloves garlic, minced
- 4 tablespoons cornstarch dissolved in 8 tablespoons water
- Pinch salt
- Ground pepper
- Sesame seeds

Preparation

1. Sprinkle slow cooker with cooking spray.
2. Season chicken with salt on both sides and place on the bottom of the slow cooker

3. In a small bowl add honey, soy sauce, onion, ketchup, oil, garlic, and mix well. Pour over chicken.
4. Cook on low for 3-4 hours or until chicken cooked.
5. Remove chicken from the cooker and leave sauce. Dissolve cornstarch in the water and pour into the slow cooker. Mix with sauce.
6. Cook sauce on high for 10-15 minutes or until slightly thickened.
7. Cut chicken into medium pieces, return to the pot and dip in a sauce before serving.
8. Season with sesame seeds and serve with cooked rice.

Sweet Chicken Breast with Honey

Ingredients

- 1 pound chicken breast, skinless
- ¼ teaspoon ground pepper
- ½ cup honey
- ¼ cup soy sauce
- ½ teaspoon salt
- 1 onion, chopped
- 1/8 cup ketchup
- 1 tablespoon vegetable oil
- 1 clove garlic, minced
- ¼ teaspoon red pepper flakes

Preparation

1. Season chicken breasts in both sides with salt and pepper. Put into the slow cooker.
2. In the medium bowl mix soy sauce, honey, chopped onion, ketchup, garlic, and pepper flakes. Pour over chicken with mixture.
3. Cook on low for at least 3 hours.

4. Cut cooked chicken into bite size pieces, return to the crockpot and cover with sauce.

Famous Santa Fe Chicken

Ingredients

- 1 ½ pounds chicken breast, skinless
- 1 can (14 oz) tomatoes with green chilies, diced
- 1 can (14 oz) black beans
- 6-8 oz frozen corn
- ½ cup fresh cilantro, chopped
- 1 can (14 oz) chicken broth
- 2 shallot, chopped
- 1 teaspoon garlic powder
- 1 teaspoon onion powder
- 1 teaspoon cumin
- 1 teaspoon cayenne pepper
- Salt and pepper for seasoning

Preparation

1. In the large bowl add chicken broth, beans, corn, tomatoes, cilantro, shallot, garlic and onion powders, cumin, cayenne pepper, salt, and stir to combine.
2. Place this mixture in the slow cooker.

3. Season chicken breasts and lay them on the top of other ingredients inside the crockpot.
4. Cook on low for 8-10 hours.
5. In an hour before serving remove chicken from the slow cooker and shred.
6. Return chicken into the slow cooker and stir with other ingredients.
7. Serve and season with salt and pepper to taste.

Amazing Tender Chicken with Mushrooms

Ingredients

- 1 ½ pounds chicken breasts, skinless and trimmed of fat
- 2 cups chicken broth
- 1 middle onion, minced
- 6 cloves garlic, minced
- 1 tablespoon Olive Oil
- 1 tablespoon tomato paste
- 1 teaspoon dried thyme, crushed
- 1 lb fresh mushrooms, sliced
- 2 tablespoons white wine vinegar
- 2 tablespoons quick-cooking tapioca
- ½ cup Parmesan cheese
- 1 tablespoon dried parsley
- Salt and pepper for seasoning

Preparation

1. In microwave-safe bowl mix onion, garlic, olive oil, tomato paste, thyme. Cook for about 5 minutes until onion becomes tender. Pour into a slow cooker.
2. Season chicken with salt and pepper.
3. In a bowl stir the chicken breasts, mushrooms, broth, vinegar and tapioca and put the mixture in the slow cooker.
4. Cover and cook on low for 4-6 hours.
5. Remove the chicken and shred it into large pieces using two forks. (By the way, this is optional, maybe someone wants to leave the whole piece).
6. Remove extra fat from the surface and place the chicken back into the crockpot.
7. Add cheese and dried parsley.
8. Season to taste and serve with pasta or rice.

Zucchini and Tomato Spicy Pasta Sauce

Ingredients

- 2 cups zucchini, shredded
- 4 oz mushrooms, chopped
- ½ medium onion, chopped
- 4-5 medium tomatoes, diced
- 1 bay leaf
- ¼ cup fresh parsley, chopped
- 4 garlic cloves, minced
- ¼ teaspoon pepper
- 1 teaspoon garlic salt
- 1 teaspoon oregano
- 1 teaspoon basil
- 2 cans (8 oz) tomato sauce
- 2 tablespoon quick-cooking tapioca
- 1 pound turkey sausage (optional, you can cook both with or without meat)

Preparation
1. Combine all vegetables in the large bowl.
2. Add spices, stir to combine.
3. Add everything in the slow cooker, cover and cook on low for 6-8 hours.
4. Stir and add sausages.
5. Season to taste and serve over pasta or spaghetti in your choice.

Adorable Crockpot Italian Chicken

Ingredients

- 2-4 chicken breasts, boneless and skinless
- 1 package (8 oz) cream cheese, softened
- 1 can cream of chicken soup
- 1 package Italian dressing seasoning
- Pasta or rice to serve

Preparation

1. Prepare chicken and place in the slow cooker.
2. Combine softened cream cheese, cream of chicken and Italian seasoning and place evenly over the chicken.
3. Cover and cook on high up to 5 hours or until chicken will be prepared and fully tender.
4. Serve over cooked pasta or rice.

Slow Cooker Hawaiian Chicken with Pineapple

Ingredients

- 5-6 chicken breast, skinless and boneless
- ½ cup ketchup
- ½ teaspoon Worcestershire sauce
- 1 teaspoon mustard
- ½ pineapple with juice, crushed
- ½ cup brown sugar
- 1 can pineapple chunks

Preparation

1. Prepare chicken breasts.
2. In large bowl mix ketchup, Worcestershire sauce, mustard, crushed pineapple with juice, brown sugar. Stir to combine.
3. Dip chicken breasts to the mixture and put them into the slow cooker.
4. Cover and cook on high for 4-6 hours or until chicken tender.

5. For the last 30 minutes of cooking time open the crockpot and dump in pineapple chunks.
6. Serve over rice or as you like.

Bacon Cheese Potatoes

Ingredients

- ¼ pound bacon, diced
- 2-3 medium onion, sliced
- 5 medium potatoes, sliced
- ½ pound cheddar cheese, sliced
- 1 tablespoon butter
- Salt and ground pepper for seasoning
- Green onion (optional)

Preparation

1. Put foil on the bottom of the slow cooker, leaving enough to cover the potatoes.
2. Make a layer half of potatoes, bacon, onion and cheese. Season with salt and pepper to taste and dot with butter.
3. Do the same layers with the rest of ingredients. Season to taste and dot with butter.
4. Cover everything with remaining foil.
5. Cover and cook on low for 8-10 hours.

Tender Pork Chops

Ingredients

- 4 pork loin chops (4 oz in each), boneless
- 1 can (14 oz) chicken broth
- ¾ cup all-purpose flour, divided
- ½ teaspoon ground mustard
- ½ teaspoon garlic pepper blend
- 2 tablespoon canola oil
- Salt for seasoning

Preparation

1. Take 1 large plastic bag. Put in it ½ cup flour, mustard, garlic pepper, salt.
2. Add pork chops, one at a time. Shake well to be sure that meat covers evenly.
3. Brown pork in a large skillet in oil on both sides.
4. Put browned pork chops to the slow cooker.
5. Place remaining flour in a bowl, add chicken broth. Whisk until smooth.
6. Pour this mixture over chops.

7. Cover and cook on low for 3-4 hours or until meat is tender.
8. Serve until warm.
9. Enjoy.

Delicious Chicken Cordon Bleu

Ingredients

- 6 chicken breast halves, boneless and skinless
- 10 oz condensed cream of chicken soup
- 1 cup milk
- 4 oz ham, sliced
- 4 oz Swiss cheese, sliced
- 8 oz herbed dry breadcrumbs
- ¼ cut butter, melted

Preparation

1. In a small bowl combine condensed cream of chicken soup and milk.
2. Pour enough soup into the slow cooker to cover the bottom.
3. Lay chicken breasts over the sauce.
4. Cover with ham and Swiss cheese slices.
5. Pour the remaining soup mixture over the layers, trying to distribute between layers.
6. Sprinkle herbed breadcrumbs on top, drizzle with butter over breadcrumbs.

7. Cover with lid and cook on low for 5-6 hours.

Tender Beef Stroganoff

Ingredients
- 2 pounds stew beef
- ½ cup beef broth
- 16 oz fresh mushrooms, sliced
- 2 packages onion soup mix
- 3 tablespoon Worcestershire sauce
- 2 ½ cup sour cream
- 4 oz cream cheese, softened
- 1 package cooked egg noodles for serving

Preparation:
1. Put stew meat, broth, sliced mushrooms, soup mix, Worcestershire sauce into the crockpot and cook on low for 4-6 hours until meat prepared.'
2. After that add sour cream and cream cheese into the cooker, stir the mixture until combined and smooth.
3. Serve over cooked egg noodles.
4. Enjoy.

Soups & Stews

German Classic Sauerkraut Soup

Ingredients

- 1 potato cut into small cubes
- 1 pound smoked sausages cut into ½ inch cubes
- 1 can (32 oz)sauerkraut, rinsed and drained
- 4 cups chicken broth
- 1 can (10 oz) condensed cream of mushroom soup
- ½ pound fresh mushrooms, sliced
- 1 cup cooked chicken, cubed
- 2 carrots, sliced
- 2 celery ribs, sliced
- 2 tablespoon dill
- ½ teaspoon ground pepper
- 3-5 bacon strips, cooked

Preparation

1. Prepare all ingredients, wash and dry vegetables.
2. Combine all ingredients in the slow cooker, pour over with chicken broth.

3. Cover and cook on high for 5 hours until vegetables become tender.
4. Skim extra fat.
5. Garnish with crumbled bacon and enjoy.

Chicken Soup with Spinach and Herbs

Ingredients

- 1 pound chicken things, boneless and skinless, cut into ½ inch pieces
- 1 can (16 oz) kidney beans, rinsed and well drained
- 14 oz chicken broth
- 1 onion, chopped
- 1 sweet red pepper, chopped
- 2 tablespoons tomato paste
- 3 garlic cloves, minced
- ½ teaspoon fresh rosemary, minced
- ½ teaspoon fresh thyme, minced
- ½ teaspoon dried oregano, crushed
- ¼ teaspoon salt
- ¼ teaspoon pepper
- 3 cups fresh baby spinach
- ¼ cup Parmesan cheese, shredded

Preparation
1. Prepare all ingredients.
2. Combine them in the slow cooker, cover and cook on low for 4-5 hours or until chicken is tender.
3. Stir in baby spinach.
4. Cover and cook for 30 minutes until spinach is wilted.
5. Top with cheese.

Mom's Amazing Pot Roast

Ingredients

- 1 pound pot roast
- 3 cubes beef bouillon
- 10 oz beef broth
- 3 garlic cloves, minced
- ¼ teaspoon, Cayenne pepper
- 2 tablespoon cumin
- 1 teaspoon oregano
- ¼ teaspoon ground pepper
- 2 middle carrots, grated

Preparation

1. Cut meat into 2-3 inch cubes and place into the slow cooker.
2. Combine beef broth, bouillon cubes, garlic, cayenne pepper, cumin, oregano and ground pepper.
3. Pour this mixture over the meat in the crockpot.
4. Cover and cook on high for 3-4 hours or until meat ready and tender.
5. Serve with rice or potatoes.

Salsa Verde Pork

Ingredients

- 2 pounds pork sirloin or loin
- 1 jar (16 oz) Salsa Verde
- 1 can (4 oz) green chilies, diced
- 1 tablespoon ground cumin
- Salt for seasoning

Preparation

1. Spray slow cooker with cooking spray.
2. Freely sprinkle salt over pork. Place meat to the cooker.
3. Pour a jar of Salsa Verde over pork. Then add diced green chilies and sprinkle with ground cumin.
4. Cover the crock pot and cook on low for at least 8 hours.
5. Shred pork and put back to the sauce.
6. You may serve with any topping you like: cheese, sour cream, tomatoes, etc.
7. Enjoy!

Potato Stew with Vegetables and Spices

Ingredients

- 3 pounds potatoes, diced
- 1 medium onion, minced
- 4 medium tomatoes
- 2 teaspoon mustard seeds
- 1 teaspoon ground ginger
- 1 teaspoon garam masala
- 1 teaspoon turmeric
- ½ teaspoon ground cumin
- ½ teaspoon chili powder
- ¼ cup dried chili flakes
- 3 tablespoon Olive oil
- Salt and ground black pepper to taste

Preparation

1. In a bowl mix spices expect of mustard seeds: ginger, garam masala, turmeric, cumin, chili powder.

2. Prepare vegetables, wash, peel and cube potatoes, mince onion.
3. Wash tomatoes, squeeze out seeds and chop them into little pieces.
4. Hit some olive oil, add mustard seeds and cook until popping.
5. Add onion; cook for near 5 minutes until transparent.
6. Add spices and cook for 3-4 minutes to get the flavor going.
7. Add cubed potatoes. Stir and make sure that every cube gets into spice mixture.
8. Add diced tomatoes.
9. Salt and add some ground pepper to taste.
10. Cook for at least 4-6 hours or until ready.

Cooking Measurement Conversions

Liquid Measures

1 gal = 4 qt = 8 pt = 16 cups = 128 fl oz
½ gal = 2 qt = 4 pt = 8 cups = 64 fl oz
¼ gal = 1 qt = 2 pt = 4 cups = 32 fl oz
½ qt = 1 pt = 2 cups = 16 fl oz
¼ qt = ½ pt = 1 cup = 8 fl oz

Dry Measures

1 cup = 16 Tbsp = 48 tsp = 250ml
¾ cup = 12 Tbsp = 36 tsp = 175ml
⅔ cup = 10 ⅔ Tbsp = 32 tsp = 150ml
½ cup = 8 Tbsp = 24 tsp = 125ml
⅓ cup = 5 ⅓ Tbsp = 16 tsp = 75ml
¼ cup = 4 Tbsp = 12 tsp = 50ml
⅛ cup = 2 Tbsp = 6 tsp = 30ml
1 Tbsp = 3 tsp = 15ml

Dash or Pinch or Speck = less than ⅛ tsp

Quickies

1 fl oz = 30 ml
1 oz = 28.35 g
1 lb = 16 oz (454 g)
1 kg = 2.2 lb
1 quart = 2 pints

U.S.	Canadian
¼ tsp	1.25 mL
½ tsp	2.5 mL
1 tsp	5 mL
1 Tbl	15 mL
¼ cup	50 mL
⅓ cup	75 mL
½ cup	125 mL
⅔ cup	150 mL
¾ cup	175 mL
1 cup	250 mL
1 quart	1 liter

Recipe Abbreviations

Cup = c or C
Fluid = fl
Gallon = gal
Ounce = oz
Package = pkg
Pint = pt
Pound = lb or #
Quart = qt
Square = sq
Tablespoon = T or Tbl or TBSP or TBS
Teaspoon = t or tsp

*Some measurements were rounded

Fahrenheit (°F) to Celcius (°C)

$°C = (°F - 32) \times 5/9$

°F	°C
32°F	0°C
40°F	4°C
140°F	60°C
150°F	65°C
160°F	70°C
225°F	107°C
250°F	121°C
275°F	135°C
300°F	150°C
325°F	165°C
350°F	177°C
375°F	190°C
400°F	205°C
425°F	220°C
450°F	230°C
475°F	245°C
500°F	260°C

OVEN TEMPERATURES

WARMING: 200°F
VERY SLOW: 250°F - 275°F
SLOW: 300°F - 325°F
MODERATE: 350°F - 375°F
HOT: 400°F - 425°F
VERY HOT: 450°F - 475°F

Copyright 2016 by Colin Rivera - All rights reserved.

No part of this publication may be reproduced or transmitted in any form or by any means, mechanical or electronic, including photocopying and recording, or by any information storage and retrieval system, without permission, in written, from the author.

All attempts have been made to verify information provided in this publication. Neither the author nor the publisher assumes any responsibility for errors or omissions of the subject matter herein. This publication is not intended for use as a source of legal or accounting advice. The Publisher wants to stress that the information contained herein may be subject to varying state and/or local laws or regulations. All users are advised to retain competent counsel to determine what state and/or local laws or regulations may apply to the user's particular business.

The purchaser or reader of this publication assumes responsibility for the use of these materials and information. Adherence to all applicable laws and regulations, federal, state, and local, governing professional licensing, business practices, advertising, and all other aspects of doing business in the United States or any other jurisdiction is the sole responsibility of the purchaser or reader.

The author and Publisher assume no responsibility or liability whatsoever on the behalf of any purchaser or reader of these materials for injury due to use of any of the methods contained herein. Any perceived slights of specific people or organizations are unintentional.

Wait a Minute ...

Are you going to buy an **Air Fryer** but do not know how to use it?

Or you already bought it and your **Air Fryer** now gathering dust on a shelf?

>>> Hurry up, and get my new Air Fryer Cookbook on Amazon <<<

Conclusion

I hope this book has helped you realize how essential role played the slow cooker in preparing delicious and tasty dishes. And if you like cooking and do not want waste your time in the kitchen, using the crock pot at home is the right choice.

As you understand from this cookbook there are a lot of dishes you can cook with the help of the slow cooker. But you always can create your own dishes, combining your favorite ingredients.

Enjoy healthy stew food with minimum oil and salt at your home!

Made in the USA
Lexington, KY
28 June 2017